Yuletide Blessings

Christmas
Stories
that Warm
the Heart

B&H
PUBLISHING GROUP
Nashville, Tennessee

Nan Corbitt Allen

Dedication

To my husband, Dennis, who tempers my angst and chronic discouragement with genuine love, optimism, patience, and affirmation. I love you.

To my sons and their wives who are living proof that God's hand has poured out His richest blessings on my life. I love you.

To my grandchildren who remind me that it can be like Christmas everyday. I love you!

To all who will buy this book—thank you! Now buy several more and give them away so you can experience the joy of blessing someone else.

Contents

Stories Behind the Carols

Tales of Yore

Classic Holiday Shows

Your Own Christmas Story

Introduction

Traditions. Trends. There are lots of both when it comes to the celebration of Christmas.

A trend might contain traditions.

For instance, the Christmas tree has been around for centuries, but even in my lifetime this holiday icon has given in to the trends. I remember those days when we put silver cellophane icicles on our Christmas trees. Oh, how I loved to throw them haphazardly at the boughs only to be scolded for not draping them neatly over each branch! And then there was the aluminum tree phrase, complete with a spotlight and a revolving color wheel in front of it. Blue. Red. Green. Amber. You didn't have to choose a color scene. It was chosen for you every fifteen seconds. Somewhere after that, our family transitioned into a solid white artificial tree with a black light beaming up at it. Hey, it was the '60s. My sister and I wondered if it could be seen from outer space.

This book will hopefully unwrap a few traditions, legends, and myths that come to the surface during this season. But more important, unfold some amazing truths about the first Christmas.

I pray it will bless you (as the title implies) and that you will be able to bless someone else with the gift of this book—containing the writing of your own story on the last few pages.

"Bless the LORD, O my soul: and all that is within me, bless his holy name." (Ps. 103:1 KJV)

The Real Christmas Story

They Foretold Us So

They were called prophets because they could foretell the future by divine revelation. Joel, Jonah, Amos, Isaiah, Micah, Nahum, Zephaniah, Jeremiah, Habakkuk—just to name a few. These were designated mouthpieces for God who told the world what He wanted said. Many times that included promises of events that would happen in the future, oftentimes a thousand years or so later.

And there were others who weren't really numbered among the prophets but who wrote prophetic words from God. King David, for instance, wrote prophecies in his song lyrics.

Most scholars agree that there are more than three hundred Old Testament prophecies that predicted the coming of the Messiah. When you read them and then compare those to events recorded in the New Testament that are obvious fulfillments of the prophecies, it's truly amazing to see God's plan revealed.

Here are a few of the prophecies concerning just the *coming* of Jesus and how they were fulfilled thousands of years later. Let's start with Isaiah who predicted how the Messiah would come, who He would be, and even where He would grow up.

"Therefore, the Lord Himself will give you a sign: The virgin will conceive, have a son, and name him Immanuel." (Isa. 7:14)

"'She will give birth to a son, and you are to name Him Jesus, because He will save His people from their sins.' Now all this took place to fulfill what was spoken by the Lord through the prophet: 'See, the virgin will become pregnant and give birth to a son, and they will name Him Immanuel, which is translated 'God is with us.'" (Matt. 1:18–23)

The Real Christmas Story

"The surviving remnant of the house of Judah will again take root downward and bear fruit upward." (Isa. 37:31)

"The historical record of Jesus Christ, the Son of David, the Son of Abraham: Abraham fathered Isaac, Isaac fathered Jacob, Jacob fathered Judah and his brothers, and Jacob fathered Joseph the husband of Mary, who gave birth to Jesus who is called the Messiah." (Matt. 1:1–4, 14)

Micah spoke about where Messiah would be born.

"Bethlehem Ephrathah, you are small among the clans of Judah; One will come from you to be ruler over Israel for Me. His origin is from antiquity, from eternity." (Micah 5:2)

"And Joseph also went up from the town of Nazareth in Galilee, to Judea, to the city of David, which is called Bethlehem, because he was of the house and family line of David, to be registered along with Mary, who was engaged to him and was pregnant. While they were there, the time came for her to give birth. Then she gave birth to her firstborn Son, and she wrapped Him snugly in cloth and laid Him in a

feeding trough—because there was no room for them at the lodging place." (Luke 2:4–6)

Hosea chimed in about a journey that Jesus and His family would take to protect Him from Herod's wrath.

"When Israel was a child, I loved him, and out of Egypt I called My son." (Hosea 11:1)

"So he (Joseph) got up, took the child and His mother during the night, and escaped to Egypt. He stayed there until Herod's death, so that what was spoken by the Lord through the prophet might be fulfilled: Out of Egypt I called My Son." (Matt. 2:14–15)

These are just a few of the amazing prophecies that were fulfilled and only these are about His birth and childhood. Hundreds more predict specifics about His teaching, His healing ministry, His arrest, His trial, His execution, and His resurrection.

It seems God had a plan all along and He let His people in on it a little piece at a time. When all the pieces are assembled (prophecy to fulfillment), it paints a beautiful picture of the Incarnate God and His redemptive plan.

The Real Christmas Story

This season look for the single threads, either from Scripture or from direct revelation, that together weave a tapestry of how much God loves you and wants you to know Him.

"May you be blessed by the LORD, the Maker of heaven and earth." (Ps. 115:15)

Everybody's Hometown

O little town of Bethlehem

How still we see thee lie

Above thy deep and dreamless sleep

The silent stars go by

Yet in thy dark streets shineth

The everlasting Light

The hopes and fears of all the years

Are met in thee tonight

Bethlehem. It was a little town. The population when Jesus was born there was a little over three hundred people. Its name means "house of bread" in Hebrew and it was perhaps so named because the surrounding area was a flourishing grain-producing area in Old Testament times.

The town was and is still located five miles south west of Jerusalem. The big city of Jerusalem was sort of the hub for the Jews for centuries. King Solomon built the first permanent temple and his palace there. It would be significant to Christians later since it would be the place where Jesus was imprisoned, tried, crucified, buried, and resurrected. So why not select the holy city of Jerusalem (and not Bethlehem) to be the first to cradle God's only begotten Son? Why does the little town of Bethlehem seem to hold such a special place in God's heart?

Maybe something in Bethlehem's rich history will answer the question.

The town is first mentioned in Genesis 35. Jacob, whom God renamed Israel, buried his beloved wife, Rachel there.

> *"They set out from Bethel. When they were still some distance from Ephrath, Rachel began to give birth, and her labor was difficult. During her difficult labor, the midwife said to her, 'Don't be afraid, for you have another son.' With her last breath—for she was dying—she named him Ben-oni, but his father called him Benjamin. So Rachel died and was buried on the way to Ephrath (that is, Bethlehem). Jacob set up a marker on her grave; it is the marker at Rachel's grave to this day." (Gen. 35:16–20)*

So, Bethlehem became a place of grief or bittersweet endings.

It was the birthplace and site of David's anointing as Israel's second king.

"The Lord said to Samuel, 'I am sending you to Jesse of Bethlehem because I have selected a king from his sons.'" (1 Sam. 16:1)

So, the town had some royal roots.

The prophet Micah revealed that the Son of God would be born there.

"Bethlehem Ephrathah, you are small among the clans of Judah; One will come from you to be ruler over Israel for Me. His origin is from antiquity, from eternity." (Mic. 5:2)

Bethlehem was selected several centuries before as the birthplace of the Messiah long before the birth happened.

It had a divine appointment.

Still, why Bethlehem? It was not particularly special historically, economically, or spiritually.

Many have surmised that the Lord wanted to identify with the common, the ordinary and so He chose a common ordinary town as the site of His Son's birth. Others have said that "the House of Bread" moniker is an indication that Jesus was to be the "Bread of Life". After all, Jesus said,

> *"I am the bread of life . . . No one who comes to Me will ever be hungry, and no one who believes in Me will ever be thirsty again." (John 6:35)*

All of these may be among the reasons God chose the little town of Bethlehem. And then again, His choice may have nothing to do with these. All we know is that God set aside that town at that time for the Holy Nativity.

Phillips Brooks, who wrote the lyrics to "O Little Town of Bethlehem," was in Bethlehem Christmas Eve, 1865. He recalls that night.

> I remember standing in the old church in Bethlehem, close to the spot where Jesus was born, when the whole church was ringing hour after hour with splendid hymns of praise to God, how again and again it seemed as if I could hear voices I knew well, telling each other of the Wonderful Night of the Savior's birth.

The hopes and fears of all the years were indeed met in one holy Child born there on one holy night.

And Now a Word from Heaven

They appear six times in the biblical Christmas story either one at a time or as an army. Since angels in the Bible were mostly messengers from God to people on earth, they played a huge part in bringing the message of Christ's birth.

First, one angel named Gabriel had a conversation with a Jewish priest named Zachariah. Zachariah and his wife, Elizabeth had served God faithfully for many years but had never had children of their own. One day as Zachariah was on temple duty offering sacrifices to God, Gabriel appeared to him. The conversation went like this:

"Do not be afraid, Zechariah, because your prayer has been heard. Your wife Elizabeth will bear you a son, and you will name him John. There will be joy and delight for you, and many will rejoice at his birth. For he will be great in the sight of the Lord and will never drink wine or beer. He will be filled with the Holy Spirit while still in his mother's womb. He will turn many of the sons of Israel to the Lord their

God. And he will go before Him in the spirit and power of Elijah, to turn the hearts of fathers to their children, and the disobedient to the understanding of the righteous, to make ready for the Lord a prepared people."

"How can I know this?" Zechariah asked the angel. "For I am an old man, and my wife is well along in years."

The angel answered him, "I am Gabriel, who stands in the presence of God, and I was sent to speak to you and tell you this good news. Now listen! You will become silent and unable to speak until the day these things take place, because you did not believe my words, which will be fulfilled in their proper time."
(Luke 1:13–20)

The conversation ended abruptly since Zechariah could not speak for a few months, but Gabriel's words began Jesus' story. The angel was announcing Jesus' forerunner (and cousin) John the Baptist. John's purpose was to preach repentance to God's people before Jesus' public ministry began. In other words, John the Baptist came to prepare the way for Christ's purpose to teach about God and then to offer Himself as a sacrifice for the sins of the world.

The second appearance of an angel was to Mary, the soon-to-be-mother of Jesus. This, too, was a conversation with Gabriel. It went like this:

"Rejoice, favored woman! The Lord is with you."

But she was deeply troubled by this statement, wondering what kind of greeting this could be.

Then the angel told her: "Do not be afraid, Mary, for you have found favor with God. Now listen: You will conceive and give birth to a son, and you will call His name Jesus. He will be great and will be called the Son of the Most High, and the Lord God will give Him the throne of His father David. He will reign over the house of Jacob forever, and His kingdom will have no end.

Mary asked the angel, "How can this be, since I have not been intimate with a man?"

The angel replied to her: "The Holy Spirit will come upon you, and the power of the Most High will overshadow you. Therefore, the holy One to be born will be called the Son of God. And consider your relative Elizabeth—even she has conceived a son in her old age, and this is the sixth month for her who was called childless. For nothing will be impossible with God."

"I am the Lord's slave," said Mary. "May it be done to me according to your word." (Luke 1:28–38)

Notice that Mary made the same argument with the angel as Zechariah, but Gabriel took a more gentle approach this time. He simply used God's power as an explanation, and Mary immediately is satisfied with his answer.

The next appearance was to Joseph, Mary's fiancé. But this time the angel (not named here) appears in a dream with these words:

"Joseph, son of David, don't be afraid to take Mary as your wife, because what has been conceived in her is by the Holy Spirit. She will give birth to a son, and you are to name Him Jesus, because He will save His people from their sins."

When Joseph got up from sleeping, he did as the Lord's angel had commanded him. He married her but did not know her intimately until she gave birth to a son. And he named Him Jesus." (Matt. 1:20–21, 24–25)

Simple enough. Short and sweet.

Months later, after John the Baptist had been born and just after Jesus had arrived, an angel appears out of the blue to shepherds who were keeping sheep in a field near Bethlehem. No dialogue this time, perhaps because the poor shepherds were too shocked to protest or ask questions. This was not a conversation but a proclamation.

> *"For unto you is born this day in the city of David a Saviour, which is Christ the Lord. And this shall be a sign unto you; Ye shall find the babe wrapped in swaddling clothes, lying in a manger.'" (Luke 2:11–12 KJV)*

Before the guys could gather their things and obey the angel's command God opened up the heavens and spilled out a huge army of angels that proclaimed:

> *"Glory to God in the highest heaven, and peace on earth to people He favors!" (v. 14)*

The shepherds were able to gather their wits enough to get up and go straight to Bethlehem where they found the Child just as the angel had said.

The next two angelic appearances before the nativity story completely closes are to Joseph again both times in a dream. The Child was in danger from Herod's edict to get rid of anyone who might threaten his throne. The angel said,

> *"Get up! Take the child and His mother, flee to Egypt, and stay there until I tell you. For Herod is about to search for the child to destroy Him." (Matt. 2:13)*

Some time later, after Herod's death, Joseph had another angel dream. This time it was:

> *"Get up! Take the child and His mother and go to the land of Israel, because those who sought the child's life are dead." (Matt. 2:20)*

Joseph wins the prize for the most single appearances but the shepherds lead in seeing the most angels at one time.

Though angels sometimes brought bad news from heaven, this time the news was the best news ever!

This season communicate one-on-one or with an army of other messengers . . .

> *"Arise, shine, for your light has come, and the glory of the Lord shines over you." (Isa. 60:1)*

Shepherds Abiding

In the same region, shepherds were staying out in the fields and keeping watch at night over their flock. Then an angel of the Lord stood before them, and the glory of the Lord shone around them, and they were terrified. But the angel said to them, "Don't be afraid, for look, I proclaim to you good news of great joy that will be for all the people: Today a Savior, who is Messiah the Lord, was born for you in the city of David. This will be the sign for you: You will find a baby wrapped snugly in cloth and lying in a feeding trough."

Suddenly there was a multitude of the heavenly host with the angel, praising God and saying:

Glory to God in the highest heaven, and peace on earth to people He favors!

When the angels had left them and returned to heaven, the shepherds said to one another, "Let's go straight to Bethlehem and see what has happened, which the Lord has made known to us." (Luke 2:8–15)

⭐ Abraham ⭐ Amos ⭐ Moses
⭐ Jacob ⭐ David ⭐ Joseph

This is a partial roll call of shepherds mentioned in the Bible. Quite an impressive list!

However, by the time Jesus was born in Bethlehem, sheepherding, as an occupation, was not considered a high-class job. In fact, history tells us that shepherds were mostly shunned in Jewish society by the time Jesus was born.

So why were the shepherds personally invited to be the first eyes to see the King of kings? It's anybody's guess. But here are some facts about shepherds and their sheep in that time, and perhaps you can draw your own conclusions:

The Men

They most likely lived out in the fields. Their roof was a canopy of stars and their bed was a carpet of dew-laden grass.

The qualifications for being a shepherd don't seem so tough until you look at what could be required of them.

They had to be on a constant watch for new grazing lands and watering holes, for once one pasture was bare or a stream had gone dry, someone had to scout out fresh grass and a new source of water. Once they found fresh pastures, they also had to protect those lands from other grazers. Establishing territory meant having to defend pastures. Predators, like lions, bears, jackals, and hyenas, were constant threats to a flock, and a shepherd would have to resort to hand-to-hand combat as his only defense at times. A hired shepherd had to account for every sheep and if even one sheep was missing it had to be recovered or the shepherd would have to pay the flock's owner for it.

The Sheep

Sheep and goats were vital to the culture and economy of people in biblical times. Early on, the herds mostly belonged to nomadic tribes, so the owners and their families probably wrangled their own livestock. These animals provided milk (which could be made into yogurt, butter, and cheese), wool (which could be weaved into fabric), and of course, they provided meat. Horns from the males were used as containers for oil, and one day somebody figured out that they could blow on one end of the horn and make music. The first trumpet! In the Old Testament they were called *shofars*. So sheep and goats provided food, clothing, communication, and entertainment.

But their most notable function was their part in Jewish worship. Since the beginning of time, God had required Man to give a living sacrifice, ceremonially placed on an altar, and slaughtered. It was the worshipper's way of giving something of great value to the Lord Almighty. Sheep, goats, and oxen were almost indispensable to human existence in those days, so the sacrifice of one of them was a huge sign of surrender and obedience.

When the nomadic existence of the Israelites wound down and their cities began to pop up all over the promised land, the sheep and goats were still very much needed but they had to graze outside the city gates. That meant that someone was designated (perhaps younger sons of a large family) or hired to tend to the animals' needs. Most of the Bible translations say that the shepherds were keeping watch over their flocks. Although the shepherds were well known for their skilled and compassionate care for the sheep they tended, it's not likely that they owned them. These shepherds were almost without doubt, hired hands.

There is speculation that the sheep outside of Bethlehem the night Jesus was born were owned by the temple in Jerusalem and that the rabbis had consecrated these animals solely for sacrificial worship. However, the Scripture doesn't mention this anywhere in the account of Jesus' birth. If it is true, then the whole visitation of angels to these shepherds could have a deeper, more symbolic meaning.

The Job

February and March were lambing months. Shepherds often became "midwives" for the ewes as they gave birth. Shearing of the sheep happened at the end of the summer, and often the shepherds were paid in wool that they could then sell at market.

Though the region around Bethlehem had moderate year-round temperatures, the weather could sometimes be extreme. Cold and heat were hard on anybody exposed to those elements. Rainfall could be unrelenting at times.

Sheepherding was hard work. It required physical strength and endurance. Experience was its only training ground and many shepherds made this their lifetime careers.

So they were ordinary men. Why did they rate such a "show" as this?

Why would God have sent angels to invite them to view His Son?

It wasn't because of their religious positions. Their jobs would not allow them to attend religious rituals and feasts and they probably weren't regulars at temple worship. They perhaps weren't particularly hygienic either given their homeless status, so their presence in a public worship service would have been frowned upon.

It wasn't because of their social positions. They were likely known as common laborers and didn't have much chance to interact with townspeople. And yet the Scriptures tell us that . . .

> *They hurried off and found both Mary and Joseph, and the baby who was lying in the feeding trough. After seeing them, they reported the message they were told about this child, and all who heard it were amazed at what the shepherds said to them. But Mary was treasuring up all these things in her heart and meditating on them. The shepherds returned, glorifying and praising God for all they had seen and heard, just as they had been told. (Luke 2:16–20)*

Now, again, why would shepherds receive such an invitation? Was it symbolic of God's coming to the least important creature to show that His Son was humbling Himself to be like us? It could be. But perhaps it goes back to the angel choir's lyric.

"Glory to God in the highest heaven, and peace on earth to people He favors!"

So, assuming that these were, indeed, normal everyday work-for-hire shepherds and these were everyday off-the-rack sheep, it appears that God favors whom He favors. He chooses whom He chooses. Whether the shepherds' experience was symbolic (humble vs. great) or hyper-symbolic (the keeper of lambs would embrace the Lamb of God) this was God's choice, His way, His method, His plan. Speculation can abound, but God gave us all the information He wants us to have on this subject. The rest is up for prayerful interpretation.

Finally, questions to ponder:

Who kept the sheep while the shepherds went into town? What happened to those men after this experience? Did this sighting change their lives at all?

The Traveling Band

They appeared out of nowhere and then disappeared into thin air.

With the lack of facts about who they were and why they were a part of the scene surrounding the birth of Christ, many legends have grown through the centuries about the enigmatic wise men (also called Magi).

Here's all we know from the Bible:

After Jesus was born in Bethlehem of Judea in the days of King Herod, wise men from the east arrived unexpectedly in Jerusalem, saying, "Where is He who has been born King of the Jews? For we saw His star in the east and have come to worship Him."

When King Herod heard this, he was deeply disturbed, and all Jerusalem with him. So he assembled all the chief priests and scribes of the people and asked them where the Messiah would be born.

"In Bethlehem of Judea," they told him, "because this is what was written by the prophet:

And you, Bethlehem, in the land of Judah, are by no means least among the leaders of Judah: because out of you will come a leader who will shepherd My people Israel."

Then Herod secretly summoned the wise men and asked them the exact time the star appeared.

He sent them to Bethlehem and said, "Go and search carefully for the child. When you find Him, report back to me so that I too can go and worship Him."

After hearing the king, they went on their way. And there it was—the star they had seen in the east! It led them until it came and stopped above the place where the child was. When they saw the star, they were overjoyed beyond measure. Entering the house, they saw the child with Mary His mother, and falling to their knees, they worshiped Him. Then they opened their treasures and presented Him with gifts: gold, frankincense, and myrrh. And being warned in a dream not to go back to Herod, they returned to their own country by another route. (Matt. 2:1–12)

That's it. That's all we get from Scripture. So for the rest we have to look further and deduce a few things.

First of all, the words "magi" and "wise men" refer to the same group of men who came to Bethlehem to find the Christ Child, in spite of the fact that Bible translations differ on that point. However, these men got the title of kings (as seen in popular Christmas carols) when early Christian scholars pointed out that perhaps there were messianic prophecies that referred to these travelers.

> *May the kings of Tarshish and the coasts and islands bring tribute, the kings of Sheba and Seba offer gifts. Let all kings bow down to him, all nations serve him. (Ps. 72:10–11)*

> *Nations will come to your light, and kings to the brightness of your radiance. (Isa. 60:3)*

Who Were They?

Many legends have been associated with these guys, and many of them we have accepted as truth.

One huge myth is that there were three of them. Conjecture (or deduction) has given us that idea since there were three gifts named in the biblical account: gold, frankincense, and myrrh.

Those gifts, themselves, have been up for much speculation as to their significance. One theory is that each gift was thoughtfully chosen and has deep spiritual meaning, especially in light of who Jesus would become to the world.

Gold was a symbol of royalty. Jesus would be called King of kings.

Frankincense was incense that was a symbol of deity. He would be called Emmanuel—God With Us.

Myrrh was embalming oil. This could have been a foreshadowing of Jesus' redeeming death on the cross.

These have no proof, but are meaningful to us as believers mostly because of what we now know of Jesus' life, death, and resurrection.

Just as the nature of the gifts themselves, what happened to them after they were presented to the Christ Child also draws assumptions.

One story says that two thieves, who would later meet Jesus as they flanked Him on the crosses of Calvary, stole the gold. That one seems to be a bit of a stretch.

Another story is that Jesus kept the gifts and gave them to Judas later as part of the treasury that was misappropriated by His betrayer. Possible, I guess. Not likely.

There is also speculation that the myrrh given to Jesus was kept safe and used thirty-three years later to anoint His body for burial. A nice thought.

The most widespread myth is that Joseph sold all of the gifts to finance their escape to Egypt when evil King Herod threatened to kill all the babies in Bethlehem. This is the most practical of the folklore but the least romantic.

The men themselves were as mysterious as their unexpected visit. They are just called "wise men from the east" in Scripture without any clue as to where in the east they lived.

More conjecture.

There is some belief that these men were followers of Zoroaster—a prophet, a sage, and a magician from the eastern part of ancient Iran. This would make some sense and might explain why the wise men were called Magi, a word that has the same Greek origin as the word "magician."

Early Jewish historian, Josephus, and Greek historian, Herodotus, are among those who tell us that these were priests, perhaps Zoroastrian, who practiced astrology and interpreted dreams. These would be stargazers and therefore the appearance of a new star, that seemed to move no less, would have great importance to these scholars.

By the seventh century the legend of the "three" wise men gave them names: Gaspar, Melchior, and Balthazar.

When Did They Come?

In almost every Christmas pageant I've ever seen or directed, the wise men have proceeded into the scene and have placed their gifts at the feet of a newborn lying in a manger. It's almost certain that the Magi came years after the birth of Christ. The account in Matthew says that He was a young child and was living in a house, not a stable, and the calculations related to Herod's discovery of the presence of another King of the Jews makes it somewhere around two years later. After the wise men left Jerusalem, Herod ordered the death of all boys under the age of two, so this is a natural deduction.

As to where the wise men went after they encountered Jesus, Scripture just says that they returned to their own country (Matt. 2:12). We would love to think that they returned believers in the true God and that Jesus was His Son. We would also like to believe that they became missionaries and evangelists in the pagan world from which they came. But, of course, no one really knows.

Why Did They Come?

There is no mystery, however, (indicated in Scripture and in history) as to why these men followed a star to Bethlehem bringing gifts.

The Real Christmas Story

Entering the house, they saw the child with Mary His mother, and falling to their knees, they worshiped Him. (Matt. 2:11)

There's no question. No room for conjecture. Worship was their original intent. *"For we saw His star in the east and have come to worship Him" (Matt. 2:2).* And worship was the final act.

This Christmas, intentionally begin your journey to seek Christ in everything you do and let the journey take you to a place of worship. Don't let the trappings detour you. Bow down and lay your most precious gifts before Him.

Holy Family Travel Log

He had traveled a long way even before He was born. From Nazareth to Bethlehem was eighty miles—about a three- or four-day journey with a caravan—but a very pregnant Mary and her husband, Joseph, had to go from their home in the province of Galilee (where Nazareth was located) to Judea (where Bethlehem lay) to obey the Roman law of paying taxes and registering in a census. Scripture tells us that shortly after Mary and Joseph arrived in Bethlehem, Jesus was born.

The next family outing was probably only a day trip. Five miles separated the town of Bethlehem, where Jesus was born, and Jerusalem, where the temple was located.

Required by Jewish law, all parents of a newborn child were to present the child at the temple for a blessing by the priest and to bring an offering of purification for the mother and another offering for the redemption of the child. Being obedient Jewish parents, Mary and Joseph traveled from Bethlehem to Jerusalem forty days after Jesus' birth, which was required for a firstborn son.

> *And when the days of their purification according to the law of Moses were finished, they brought Him up to Jerusalem to present Him to the Lord (just as it is written in the law of the Lord: Every firstborn male will be dedicated to the Lord) and to offer a sacrifice (according to what is stated in the law of the Lord: a pair of turtledoves or two young pigeons). (Luke 2:22–24)*

While they were there, perhaps in a group of other new parents, an elderly man named Simeon stepped from the shadows. Simeon had been given the gift of prophecy (to be able to see things of God that others could not). God had told Simeon that he would see the Messiah in his lifetime with his own eyes. Simeon just knew that the Child lying in Mary's arms was the long-awaited One. Simeon, taking the infant Jesus in his arms, offered up this prayer:

> *Now, Master, You can dismiss Your slave in peace, as You promised. For my eyes have seen Your salvation. You have prepared it in the presence of all peoples—a light for revelation to the Gentiles and glory to Your people Israel. (Luke 2:29–32)*

The Bible says that Mary and Joseph were amazed at Simeon's words. And then as an aside, Simeon speaks privately to Mary,

"Indeed, this child is destined to cause the fall and rise of many in Israel and to be a sign that will be opposed—and a sword will pierce your own soul— that the thoughts of many hearts may be revealed." (Luke 2:34–35)

About that same time, an old woman, eighty-four years old named Anna, stepped forward. She, too, had been waiting for the Messiah and knew that this Child was He. Her words were not recorded but we know this:

At that very moment, she came up and began to thank God and to speak about Him to all who were looking forward to the redemption of Jerusalem. (Luke 2:38)

Luke says that the family went back to Nazareth but Matthew includes another family trip.

After they [the Wise Men] were gone, an angel of the Lord suddenly appeared to Joseph in a dream, saying "Get up! Take the child and His mother, flee to Egypt, and stay there until I tell you. For Herod is about to search for the child to destroy Him." So he got up, took the child and His mother during the night, and escaped to Egypt. He stayed there until

Herod's death, so that what was spoken by the Lord through the prophet might be fulfilled: Out of Egypt I called My Son. (Matt. 2:13–15)

Then another journey.

After Herod died, an angel of the Lord suddenly appeared in a dream to Joseph in Egypt, saying, "Get up! Take the child and His mother and go to the land of Israel, because those who sought the child's life are dead." So he got up, took the child and His mother, and entered the land of Israel. But when he heard that Archelaus was ruling over Judea in place of his father Herod, he was afraid to go there. And being warned in a dream, he withdrew to the region of Galilee. Then he went and settled in a town called Nazareth to fulfill what was spoken through the prophets, that He will be called a Nazarene. (Matt. 2:19–23)

There were other family trips during Jesus' life. Once a year they would travel to Jerusalem for the Passover Festival. On one of those trips, when Jesus was twelve years old, His parents accidently left Him behind in the city. It took them a day to realize He was missing from the caravan. They thought He was among other relatives and friends, but He was nowhere to be found.

Backtracking to Jerusalem, they finally found Him, after three days of searching, in the temple talking to the teachers who were amazed at Jesus' insights. Mary and Joseph must have been relieved to find Him safe and sound but Mary was upset with Him too.

> When His parents saw Him, they were astonished, and His mother said to Him, "Son, why have You treated us like this? Your father and I have been anxiously searching for You." His answer, "Why were you searching for Me?" He asked them. "Didn't you know that I had to be in My Father's house?" But they did not understand what He said to them.
>
> Then He went down with them and came to Nazareth and was obedient to them. His mother kept all these things in her heart. And Jesus increased in wisdom and stature, and in favor with God and with people. (Luke 2:48–52)

Have you ever accidently left a child or a family member behind? It's scary and embarrassing. These days are busy with holiday activities, and we can forget why we celebrate this season. Let's not leave Jesus behind.

Myths and Legends

Drummers Drumming

According to the enigmatic carol, "The Twelve Days of Christmas," it was the twelfth and last of the gifts my true love gave to me.

For some reason the drum has had a long history in legends, written or passed down, about events surrounding the birth of Christ. In the early 1700s a French composer, Bernard de La Monnoye, published a song called "Patapan" sometimes referred to as "Willie, Play Your Drum." It supposedly speaks of shepherds coming to the manger bringing simple instruments like drums and flutes to serenade the King of kings. Using onomatopoeia, the lyrics *tu-re-lu-re-lu* represent the sound of the flute, and *pat-a-pan* the sound of the drum.

Willie, bring your little drum
Robin, bring your flute and come
And be merry while you play

Tu-re-lu-re-lu
Pat-a-pat-a-pan
Come be merry while you play
On this joyous Christmas day!
When the men of olden days
To the King of kings gave praise
On the fife and drum did play

Tu-re-lu-re-lu
Pat-a-pat-a-pan
On the fife and drum did play
So their hearts were glad and gay!

God and man today become
More in tune than fife and drum
So be merry while you play

Tu-re-lu-re-lu
Pat-a-pat-a-pan

So be merry while you play
Sing and dance this Christmas Day!

The origins of the two musicians named, Willie and Robin, aren't known. Perhaps they were the names of La Monnoye's children. Though the story of the serenade is purely legend of course, the theology in rather enlightening.

God and Man today become
More in tune than fife and drum

Perhaps this is why the song incensed French priests. They alleged that the lyrics were trite and therefore mocked the biblical account of Christ's birth. After being submitted to a court of professors at the Sorbonne in Paris, Bernard's case was dismissed and the song lived on.

The theme of playing drums and other instruments for the newborn Christ Child seemed to catch on, and a twentieth-century composer and music teacher Katherine Kennicott Davis (who also published under a pseudonym C. R. W. Robinson) wrote a song originally titled "Carol of the Drum." We know it now as "The Little Drummer Boy." Still under copyright, it is a song that tells of a child who wanted so much to give something to the infant Jesus that he brought his drum to play for the Child, Mary, and Joseph. Though drumming sounds a bit inappropriate as a newborn gift, the lyric assures us that all gladly accepted it. A nod from Mary, a smile from Jesus, and the ox and lamb keeping time were indicators that this was appreciated. Again onomatopoeia was used, indicating that the drum made the sound *pa-rum-pa-pum-pum*.

The first well-known recording of "The Little Drummer Boy" was done by The Trapp Family Singers (the von Trapp family of *Sound of Music* fame). After that release the song has been recorded numerous times by the likes of Bing Crosby, Johnny Cash, and The Brady Bunch.

The idea of being poor with nothing to give to Jesus was also a theme picked up in a Christina Rossetti poem "In the Bleak Midwinter" (tune by Gustav Holst). The last verse of the poem reads:

> What can I give him, poor as I am?
> If I were a shepherd, I would bring a lamb
> If I were a Wise Man, I would do my part
> Yet what I can I give him? Give my heart

Myths and Legends

The songs and Ms. Rossetti's poem reminds us that all God wants from us is ourselves.

Love the LORD your God with all your heart, with all your soul, and with all your strength. (Deut. 6:5)

The Tradition Still Stands

"All rise!"

When a presiding judge enters a courtroom, the bailiff insists that we stand to our feet and remain standing until the judge is seated. This is out of respect for the dignity of the robe. We stand when we pledge allegiance to our flag and when we sing our national anthem out of loyalty and pride. Monarchs and heads of state around the globe would be offered such an honor as well.

So why do we stand when the "Hallelujah Chorus" is played or sung? Well, first a little background on the work from which it came.

Composer George Frederic Handel wrote *Messiah* as an Easter oratorio in 1741 and it was performed the following year in Dublin, Ireland, as a benefit concert for a charity hospital.

The work, in three parts or acts, tells the story of Jesus Christ. Beginning with the prophecies about His coming and His earthly ministry, the work moves to the second part, which begins with the passion of Christ and ends with His ascension. This is where the "Hallelujah

Chorus" is positioned in the oratorio. Part 3 finishes the story with Jesus' second coming.

In 1743 the work was presented in London for the first time. King George II of England was in attendance. The king was himself used to the accolades and signs of respect from loyal subjects, but what he did when the "Hallelujah Chorus" was being performed was unprecedented, if not outright peculiar. He stood up and remained standing throughout the piece. The audience, observing royal protocol, followed suit.

Of course, there is some conjecture as to why the king stood that night. One theory is that it was a mistake—that he had simply dozed off, heard the downbeat of the song, and woke with a start. Another is that he had been sitting for too long and was simply standing to stretch his legs. There are other theories but one that is the most endearing: King George wanted to stand and honor the King of kings and Lord of lords, as the lyric so states.

In any case, the tradition began and has continued. In fact, 100 years later, Queen Victoria of England rose from her wheelchair to honor the same King of kings and Lord of lords.

The text of this great musical masterpiece "Hallelujah Chorus" is from Revelation.

- *Hallelujah: for the Lord God omnipotent reigneth* is found in Revelation 19:6.

- *The kingdom of this world is become the kingdom of our Lord, and of his Christ; and he shall reign forever and ever* is from Revelation 11:15.

- *King of kings, and Lord of lords* can be found in Revelation 19:16.

Deck the Halls, the Walls, and All

Tradition.

It is a strong force in how we celebrate the birth of Christ in the twenty-first century. And in case you haven't heard this before, don't be shocked to find that most of our Christmas traditions have pagan roots.

When the gospel came into a culture in the first few centuries AD, the new covenant that Christ made with the world by dying and rising again no doubt had impact. Lives were changed drastically by the newfound belief. However, these same people still lived in the same cultures with their same traditions—traditions that they eventually adapted to signify their relationship with the true and living God.

The day of celebration itself (the birth of Christ) is unknown to us historically. Could Jesus have been born on December 25, the day on which we commemorate it? Certainly. Some scholars believe they can put the actual date of birth right on the twenty-fifth. Others are positive that it could not have been the birth date, and they are just as passionate in their beliefs as the other learned men and women who think otherwise. The fact is, no one really knows for sure exactly when Jesus was born. But almost all scholars agree that our Christmas season coincides with an ancient pagan celebration—Winter Solstice—(that predates Christianity) when the festivities were focused on the "rebirth" of the sun. Therefore our Christmas Day could have been an adaptation that Christians borrowed from the secular world.

Pagans are the original tree huggers—believing that gods inhabited vegetation. The Druids were the most prominent sect in the Anglo world. Evergreen trees were often decorated outdoors to pay homage to the gods who lived within them. Cutting them down and bringing them indoors would have been offensive to the deities of the Druids, so that part of the tradition probably has its origins elsewhere. In fact, the idea of cutting down a live tree and bringing it indoors began, scholars believe, in Germany in the fifteenth century. A legend names Christian Reformer Martin Luther as the initiator of decorating a Christmas tree inside, but there is no historical evidence to support that. We do know that early Christian fathers used some of the same pagan symbols but turned the interpretation of them to represent

Christ's arrival. Evergreen is a sign of eternity in pagan worship but eternal life in heaven by Christians.

The use of a live tree does point to a secular tradition, but artificial trees have grown in popularity through the last century or so and their history is even amusing. In 1930 the Addis Brush Company, which manufactured toilet bowl brushes, created an artificial Christmas tree using the same kind of bristles used in the brushes dyed green. This was the prototype of what many of us place prominently in our living rooms every December—basically a giant green toilet bowl brush.

Holly was part of the pagan tradition because it was believed to have powers to ban evil spirits from households. Since it is one of the few plants that does not die in winter, they believed that it had great influence with their gods. Christians today interpret the presence of the greenery to represent Christ's crown of thorns and the red berries His blood.

> The holly and the ivy,
> When they are both full grown,
> Of all trees that are in the wood,
> The holly bears the crown:

Yuletide Blessings

(chorus)
O, the rising of the sun,
And the running of the deer
The playing of the merry organ,
Sweet singing in the choir.

The holly bears a blossom,
As white as lily flow'r,
And Mary bore sweet Jesus Christ,
To be our dear Saviour

The holly bears a berry,
As red as any blood,
And Mary bore sweet Jesus Christ,
To do poor sinners good

The evergreen wreath dates back to Roman times. The Romans would give gifts to each other at the New Year, and often the gifts were evergreen branches intertwined to form a circle. This practice symbolized that the friendship would be unbroken and that the goddess of the evergreen would be pleased and therefore bring the recipient the gift of good health. Again Christians adapted the tradition by proclaiming that the wreath symbolized eternal life in Christ as the circle is woven to represent the unbroken promises of God to man.

Mistletoe, greenery we associate with kissing, also has a pagan history. The Druids believed that the plant had great medicinal powers (the berries of certain species are actually poisonous). They also believed that it had spiritual power as well because it remained in treetops long after the tree's leaves had fallen. At some point, mistletoe became a symbol of friendship and reconciliation. It seems that when warring factions came upon a tree with mistletoe, it was interpreted as a sign of peace. Armies would often sit down underneath a mistletoe-laden tree and make vows of peace using the gods of the plant as witnesses to the pact. Maybe that's where our tradition of kissing underneath a sprig of mistletoe came from and yet no one knows for sure.

Should these facts that reveal the pagan origins of our Christmas decorating traditions taint our celebration of Jesus' birth? Not at all! If anything, this should open our eyes to how God has revealed Himself—His nature, His promises, and intentions—long before He sent His Son. Though the pagans interpreted these signs from

God's creation as something else, we know that these were all along intended to reveal God's master plan of redemption.

> *The heavens declare the glory of God, and the sky proclaims the work of His hands. Their message has gone out to all the earth, and their words to the ends of the world. (Ps. 19:1, 4)*

Season's Greetings

The Brits started it.

In 1843 in London, England, John Callcott Horsley designed the first Christmas card. The picture on the card was controversial because it showed a family around the table toasting each other with wine. The main problem with the picture is that it included a small child also toasting with a glass of wine. Sir Henry Cole, who had commissioned Horsley to illustrate the card, was not disheartened by its mixed reviews. In fact, the trend of holiday cards became very popular quickly in England and other European countries. However, the idea didn't catch on in the United States until thirty or so years later after which it became part of the culture and Christmas tradition. Even with electronic communication taking a large chunk out of the "snail mail" business, there are still over two billion Christmas cards sent each year in America alone. The sale of commercial cards is still relatively strong but the trends are shifting back to a version of an older tradition—the homemade card. With digital cameras and home computers, many households are customizing their printed cards with photos of the family and personal greetings.

In the mid-1800s a young artist/lithographer named Nathaniel Currier from Boston teamed up with a young businessman, James Ives, and created a booming business making inexpensive lithographic prints for home wall hangings. Among their designs are very familiar winter and Christmas scenes that are now declared classics and have since appeared on millions of Christmas cards. However, Currier and Ives didn't make their fortune on idyllic winter scenes, but rather on lithographs of famous disaster scenes such as, *The Great Fire at Chicago, Awful Conflagration of the Steam Boat Lexington in Long Island Sound, Destruction of the Merrimac,* and *The Explosion Aboard the USS Princeton.*

The name most associated with the Christmas card (or any other greeting card for that matter) is, of course, Hallmark with 4.4 billion dollars in annual revenue. Early in the twentieth century, the company founded by J. C. Hall and his brothers was called Hall Brothers. They set up their headquarters in Kansas City, Missouri, and mostly produced Valentine's Day and Christmas cards. Then in 1917, when a Hall Brothers store ran out of tissue paper for wrapping gifts, they resorted to printing their own seasonal rolls of wrapping paper and that became and is still a large part of their business. In 1928 Hall Brothers became Hallmark, and in 1944 it adopted its current slogan "When you care enough to send the very best . . ."

The slogan is a reminder that one night in a Judean town, God cared enough about us to send His very best—Himself in the form of a child so that we could become His sons and daughters.

When the time came to completion, God sent His Son, born of a woman, born under the law, to redeem those under the law, so that we might receive adoption as sons. And because you are sons, God has sent the Spirit of His Son into our hearts, crying, "Abba, Father!" So you are no longer a slave but a son, and if a son, then an heir through God. (Gal. 4:4–7)

Flowers and Candy

Most legends vary in content and even intent depending on who and where they originated and how they were passed down. The legends that have followed two common sights at Christmastime are at least interesting and perhaps endearing. You decide.

The first is about the poinsettia plant that we see often around the holidays. It has a history (both fact and legend) that bears exploration and a little bit of qualification.

The facts are that the plant is native to Mexico where it grows wild in the country's southern tropical forests. Joel Roberts Poinsett who was once the U.S. ambassador to Mexico brought it to America in 1825. The name of the plant obviously got its common name from Mr. Poinsett. After he brought back some specimens of the plant to his home in South Carolina, it has been cultivated into variations on color, becoming popular and enjoyed all over the world.

The legend attached to this beautiful plant (whose leaves, not the flowers, provide the color) is indeed a myth but it is a lovely thought nonetheless.

A little girl named Maria (or some name her Pepita) so hoped to give a gift worthy of the newborn King at a Christmas Eve mass. She longed to join the processional that led to an altar where offerings would be made to honor the Infant Jesus. However, Maria, who was from a very poor family, had no gift to offer. As the service was beginning, she quickly pulled some weeds from along the road and bundled them into a crude bouquet. As she placed the humble offering on the altar, supposedly a miracle happened and the weeds began to blossom into beautiful bright red leaves. The poinsettia has since been referred to as "Flores de Noche Buena" or "Flowers of the Holy Night."

The poinsettia bears some reminders of Jesus and His redemption. First, the shape of the plant is somewhat like a star, which should remind us of the Star of Bethlehem that the Wise Men followed to find and worship Jesus. The red (the most common) variety of the plant symbolizes the blood of Christ. The white variation reminds us of Jesus' purity.

Another legend has followed a sweet treat often associated with Christmas—the candy cane.

It is said that a candy maker somewhere in Indiana wanted to make a confection that would be a Christian witness. He began with a stick of pure white molten candy and bent it into the shape of a *J*. It was allowed to harden in that shape. The candy maker then stained the white stick with red stripes.

The symbolism that this legend suggests is that the *J* shape refers to Jesus or perhaps turned the other way looks like a shepherd's crook, indicating that Christ was the Good Shepherd. The white base of the candy represents Jesus' holiness and purity. The red stripes are to remind us that Jesus shed His blood to pay our debt of sin before a holy God. There are several variations on this legend, too, some that even doubt its intent.

No matter. The Truth that has been attached to the story of the poinsettia and to the candy cane can serve to remind us of the beauty and the goodness of Jesus Christ.

Stories Behind the Carols

All Is Calm

Supposedly it was because of the church mice that had nibbled away at the organ bellows at St. Nicholas Church of Oberndorf, Austria near Salzburg, that one of the most beloved Christmas carols was written.

On Christmas Eve 1818, the parish priest Joseph Mohr was saddened to get the report from his organist and choirmaster, Franz Gruber, that the organ was unplayable for that evening's midnight service. To have no music for the traditional Christmas service was unthinkable. Father Mohr, however, calmly retrieved a poem that he had already penned and asked Franz to compose a melody that would be sung that evening as a duet. Franz played guitar as well as organ, so he took the guitar, and with a few strums had the basic tune to what we now know and love—"Silent Night, Holy Night." Father Mohr and Franz Gruber sang the song that night and also taught it to the congregation. Written in German, the poem went like this:

Stille Nacht, heilige Nacht,
Alles schläft; einsam wacht
Nur das traute hochheilige Paar.
Holder Knabe im lockigen Haar,
Schlaf in himmlischer Ruh!
Schlaf in himmlischer Ruh!

Stille Nacht, heilige Nacht,
Hirten erst kundgemacht
Durch der Engel Halleluja,
Tönt es laut von fern und nah:
Christ, der Retter ist da!
Christ, der Retter ist da!

Stille Nacht, heilige Nacht,
Gottes Sohn, o wie lacht

Lieb' aus deinem göttlichen Mund,
Da uns schlägt die rettende Stund'.
Christ, in deiner Geburt!
Christ, in deiner Geburt!

One literal translation from German to English goes like this:

Silent night, holy night
All is sleeping, alone watches
Only the close, most holy couple.
Blessed boy in curly hair,
Sleep in heavenly peace!
Sleep in heavenly peace!

Silent night, holy night,
Shepherds just informed
By the angels' hallelujah,
It rings out far and wide:
Christ the Savior is here!
Christ the Savior is here!

Silent night, holy night,
Son of God, oh how He laughs
Love out of your divine mouth,

Yuletide Blessings

Because now the hour of salvation
strikes for us.
Christ, in Thy birth!
Christ, in Thy birth!

The beauty of the song is somewhat lost in translation, so here is what we sing every Christmas season.

Silent night, holy night
All is calm all is bright
'Round yon virgin Mother and Child
Holy infant so tender and mild
Sleep in heavenly peace
Sleep in heavenly peace

Silent night, holy night,
Shepherds quake at the sight.
Glories stream from heaven afar,
Heav'nly hosts sing Alleluia;
Christ the Savior is born
Christ the Savior is born

Silent night, holy night,
Son of God, love's pure light.
Radiant beams from Thy holy face,
With the dawn of redeeming grace,

Jesus, Lord, at Thy birth
Jesus, Lord, at Thy birth

Be thankful this Christmas for mice in an organ chamber, a pastor who remembered his poem, a musician who could write a memorable melody, and a translator who gave us this beautiful adaptation of this precious carol.

My True Love

What would Christmas be without a rousing rendition of "The Twelve Days of Christmas"? And who in the crowd would know what it means?

Well, no one really knows the origin of the song, therefore its meaning remains a puzzle as well. But here is a thought (from legend) that might help you sing the song with a better understanding of Christmas itself.

In earlier times, the Christmas celebration began on December 25 (Christmas Day) and lasted until January 6 (Epiphany—the arrival of the Magi). It is those twelve days in between the two dates that allegedly sparked the idea for this song.

Some say that the song dates back to sixteenth-century England when there was heated conflict and even wars between Catholics and Protestants. The lyrics to "The Twelve Days of Christmas" were thought to be a device by which the Catholics could teach their children the catechism without reproach. Assuming there is some truth to that notion, then what were the lyrics meant to teach?

First, *true Love sent to me* was to represent God Himself and the blessings He bestowed on all believers. These are the blessings that define the meaning of Christmas.

1. *A partridge in a pear tree* represents Jesus as a compassionate Savior, as in Luke 13:34 that quotes Jesus as saying,

> *"Jerusalem, Jerusalem! She who kills the prophets and stones those who are sent to her. How often I wanted to gather your children together, as a hen gathers her chicks under her wings, but you were not willing!"*

Another version of the interpretation of this first Gift is that in ancient times a partridge (or dove) was used as a symbol of a divinely appointed King. Both versions agree, however, that the first Gift was about Jesus.

2. The *two turtledoves*, which are modern symbols of peace, represented the two testaments in the Bible—the Old Testament and the New Testament.

3. *Three French hens* could have been referring to the Trinity—God the Father, God the Son, and God the Holy Spirit. But this might also have hinted at the three gifts of the Holy Spirit found in 1 Corinthians 13:13—faith, hope, and love.

4. The *four calling birds* were supposed to teach about the four Gospels in the New Testament: Matthew, Mark, Luke, and John.

5. The *five gold rings* were the first five books of the Old Testament: Genesis, Exodus, Leviticus, Numbers, and Deuteronomy—also called the Pentateuch or the Torah.

6. *Six geese a-laying* was supposed to teach about the six days it took God to create the world.

7. *Seven swans a-swimming* could have been included to teach the seven gifts of the Holy Spirit. According to Romans 12:6–8 those are: prophecy, service, teaching, exhorting, giving, leading, and showing mercy.

8. *Eight maids a-milking* referred to the Beatitudes found in Matthew 5:3–10.

1. The poor in spirit are blessed, for the kingdom of heaven is theirs.
2. Those who mourn are blessed, for they will be comforted.
3. The gentle are blessed,
   for they will inherit the earth.
4. Those who hunger and thirst for righteousness are blessed, for they will be filled.

5. The merciful are blessed, for they will be shown mercy.

6. The pure in heart are blessed, for they will see God.

7. The peacemakers are blessed, for they will be called sons of God.

8. Those who are persecuted for righteousness are blessed, for the kingdom of heaven is theirs.

9. *Nine ladies dancing* refer, perhaps, to the nine fruit of the Spirit found in Galatians 5:22–23—love, joy, peace, patience, kindness, goodness, faith, gentleness, and self-control.

10. *Ten lords a-leaping* were referring to the Ten Commandments found in Exodus 20:

1. Do not have other gods besides Me.

2. Do not make an idol for yourself.

3. Do not misuse the name of the Lord your God.

4. Remember the Sabbath day, to keep it holy.

5. Honor your father and your mother.

6. Do not murder.

7. Do not commit adultery.

8. Do not steal.

9. Do not give false testimony against your neighbor.
10. Do not covet.

11. *Eleven pipers piping* were to testify about the eleven faithful apostles (sans Judas Iscariot, of course). They were listed in Luke 6:14–16:

1. Simon Peter
2. Andrew
3. James
4. John
5. Philip
6. Bartholomew
7. Matthew
8. Thomas
9. James, the son of Alphaeus
10. Simon called the Zealot
11. Judas, the son of James

12. *Twelve drummers drumming* were the twelve points of the Apostles' Creed.

1. I believe in God, the Father almighty, creator of heaven and earth.
2. I believe in Jesus Christ, his only Son, our Lord.

3. He was conceived by the power of the Holy Spirit and born of the Virgin Mary.

4. He suffered under Pontius Pilate, was crucified, died, and was buried. He descended into hell.

5. On the third day he rose again. He ascended into heaven, and is seated at the right hand of the Father.

6. He will come again to judge the living and the dead.

7. I believe in the Holy Spirit,

8. the holy catholic Church,

9. the communion of saints,

10. the forgiveness of sins,

11. the resurrection of the body,

12. and life everlasting.

If you actually received all the gifts in the quantity mentioned, you would receive 364 gifts total.

Whether this song was a subversive tactic sixteenth-century parents used to teach their children biblical truth or not, it can now be a way for us to remember the ultimate Gift and the Giver each Christmas.

He Heard the Bells on Christmas Day

From Henry Wadsworth Longfellow's journal:

CHRISTMAS 1861

"How inexpressibly sad are all holidays."

JULY 1862

"I can make no record of these days. Better leave them wrapped in silence. Perhaps someday God will give me peace."

CHRISTMAS 1862

"'A merry Christmas' say the children, but that is no more for me."

CHRISTMAS 1863

No journal entry.

CHRISTMAS 1864

I Heard the Bells on Christmas Day
Their old familiar carols play,
And wild and sweet the words repeat
Of peace on earth, good will to men.

I thought how, as the day had come,
The belfries of all Christendom
Had rolled along the unbroken song
Of peace on earth, good will to men.

And in despair I bowed my head:
"There is no peace on earth," I said,
"For hate is strong and mocks the song
Of peace on earth, good will to men."

Then pealed the bells more loud and deep:
"God is not dead, nor doth he sleep;
The wrong shall fail, the right prevail,
With peace on earth, good will to men."

Till, ringing singing, on its way,
The world revolved from night to day,
A voice, a chime, a chant sublime,
Of peace on earth, good will to men!

How did the great poet go from despair to silence to hope? It is no wonder that his poem "I Heard the Bells on Christmas Day" has become a beloved, classic Christmas carol. And when you know the story of Mr. Longfellow's journey, it inspires more than hope to those who grieve. It also recollects the reason for which Christ was sent to earth.

July 1861. The War Between the States had just begun and Henry, his wife Fanny, and their five children were in Cambridge, Massachusetts, in a house overlooking the Charles River. It was a hot summer and Fanny wrote in her journal "We are all sighing for the good sea breeze instead of this stifling land one filled with dust. Poor Allegra is very droopy with heat, and Edie has to get her hair in a net to free her neck from the weight."

The next day Fanny decided to cut little Edie's hair. Since it was the child's first haircut Fanny wanted to preserve a lock of the hair in wax as she had with the older children. Hoping for a breeze of relief, Fanny did not realize what a hazard she had created as she lit a wax candle to seal the hair package and then opened a window to get a breeze flowing. A gust blew in, caught the hot wax, which splattered Fanny's dress. The fabric immediately burst into flames. Panicked, Fanny began to run. She ran into Henry's study screaming for help. In his attempt to smother the flames he was badly burned on his face and hands. Fanny, however, died from her injuries. Henry could not attend his wife's funeral because of his burns. The pain was excruciating—physically and emotionally.

A home that should have been filled with joy and laughter at the next Christmas, 1861, was instead somber and silent. The cloud of mourning had not yet lifted. There was little sign of hope.

The following year, 1862, Charles Longfellow, Henry's oldest son, joined the Union Army. As the young man marched off to battle, his father feared he would never see his son again.

On Christmas 1863, Henry received the news. Charles had been wounded in battle. A bullet had passed under his shoulder blade and injured his spine. In those days, such a wound was most often crippling if not fatal.

The following Christmas 1864, though he was an invalid, Charles was still alive. There were rumors of the war's end and hope began to flicker. On Christmas Day, Henry picked up his pen and wrote the first verses of the Christmas carol "I Heard the Bells on Christmas Day."

Though total peace was somewhat elusive from a world point of view, it was possible that Christmas Day to find peace.

> *Don't worry about anything, but in everything through prayer and petition with thanksgiving, let your requests be made known to God. And the peace of God, which surpasses every thought, will guard your hearts and minds in Christ Jesus. (Phil. 4:6–7)*

Jingle All the Way

This song is hands down the most popular Christmas carol of all time—and yet it has nothing to do with Christmas. In fact, Christmas is not mentioned one time in the lyric.

Originally titled "One Horse Open Sleigh," author James Pierpont wrote this classic in 1857. The song struggled at first to be known, much less become a hit, so James changed the title to "Jingle Bells" and republished it. Unfortunately the title change did nothing for its exposure and popularity.

So how did it become such a holiday classic? First, a little information about the author:

James Pierpont was born in Boston in 1822 to John, a Unitarian pastor and poet, and his wife Mary. At the age of ten, James was sent away to a boarding school in New Hampshire and during one of his winters there wrote his mother a letter about the fun he had riding a sleigh through the snow. This paints an idyllic picture, no doubt, not to mention providing fodder for a lyric to come. However, at age fourteen, James ran away from his home and school and boarded a merchant ship called *The Shark*.

After ten or so years as a seafarer, James returned to Boston to get married and to settle down, but only for a while. James left his wife and children in the care of his father and headed out west during the California Gold Rush hoping to find his fortune there. He learned how to be a photographer and opened a shop in San Francisco, but it soon burned to the ground. Disillusioned, James returned to his family in Massachusetts and became an accomplished organist and music teacher and even began writing songs.

A few years later, James moved to Savannah, Georgia, to be organist and music director at a church where his brother was pastor. He continued composing songs: ballads, polkas, and minstrel songs, but most of us wouldn't recognize even one of them today.

In 1880, James's son renewed the copyright for "Jingle Bells," but even in the son's lifetime the song never generated much revenue.

So, why is the song so popular today?

In the late nineteenth century, the phonograph record was invented and musicians began recording Christmas songs. In 1898, the Edison Male Quartet recorded

"Jingle Bells" for the first time on an Edison cylinder, the forerunner to the plastic record of the next few decades. When radio became popular in the twentieth century, "Jingle Bells" received even more exposure. Since that time, Benny Goodman, Glenn Miller, Bing Crosby, and even barking dogs have recorded the song.

The most well-known lyrics are:

Dashing through the snow
In a one-horse open sleigh
O'er the fields we go
Laughing all the way
Bells on bobtail ring
Making spirits bright
What fun it is to ride and sing
A sleighing song tonight!

Jingle bells, jingle bells,
Jingle all the way.
Oh! what fun it is to ride
In a one-horse open sleigh.
Jingle bells, jingle bells,
Jingle all the way;
Oh! what fun it is to ride
In a one-horse open sleigh.

A bobtail was a horse that had had its tail cut short to keep it from being entangled in the reins.

The second verse is less popular but often included in the song:

A day or two ago
I thought I'd take a ride
And soon, Miss Fanny Bright
Was seated by my side,
The horse was lean and lank
Misfortune seemed his lot
He got into a drifted bank
And then we got upsot.

Jingle bells, jingle bells,
Jingle all the way.
Oh! what fun it is to ride
In a one-horse open sleigh.
Jingle bells, jingle bells,
Jingle all the way;
Oh! what fun it is to ride
In a one-horse open sleigh.

Stories Behind the Carols

Who is Miss Fanny Bright? No one knows. What does "upsot" mean? It's an archaic spelling of the word "upset" . . . and it rhymes with "lot."

James Pierpont was a bit of a rogue, a wanderer it seems, and he never found much success or notoriety in his lifetime pursuits, but his legendary efforts merry our hearts every Christmas.

Can the same be said of us? After we are gone, will our legacy bring celebration to the hearts of those we leave behind?

This book gives you a place to answer that question. For the twenty-fifth chapter of this book, write down the story of a memorable holiday and give this book to someone you love. Who knows? A poem or a lyric may one day become another generation's favorite song.

Carols for the Fireside

Two of our most popular Christmas songs to date were written during World War II by Jewish composers.

Irving Berlin, one of the most prolific twentieth-century writers, was a Russian immigrant who was a multitalented, but self-taught, musician. He could pick out melodies that he had heard or made up himself but only in one key—F# major—which includes mostly black keys on a piano. Early on he bought a "transposing piano" for $100 so that he could play his tunes in the key he knew but hear them in another. He could neither read nor write down a musical composition but he found others who could notate his songs for him.

A gifted writer and singer, he composed some of last century's most successful commercial hits including "Alexander's Ragtime Band," "There's No Business Like Show Business," "Easter Parade," "God Bless America," and of course, "White Christmas." Written in 1940 in sunny Southern California, "White Christmas" has a verse that describes a longing to be up north to see the white stuff, but we hardly ever sing that part. The chorus is what we all know and love.

In 1942 the film *Holiday Inn* introduced the song, sung by singer/actor Bing Crosby. Crosby's recording of the song is one of the best-selling single records of all time. It then became the title song for one of America's favorite holiday movies released in 1954.

The other favorite holiday fireside song has had two official titles: first, "Merry Christmas to You," and finally "The Christmas Song," but it's commonly referred to by the first line of the lyric, "Chestnuts Roasting on an Open Fire." Another Russian Jewish composer named Mel Tormé wrote it in 1944. He actually collaborated on the song with a lyricist named Bob Wells after he saw four lines scribbled in pencil on a notepad. They were "Chestnuts roasting," "Jack Frost nipping," "Yuletide carols," "Folks dressed up like Eskimos." The song was reportedly written in forty-five minutes and Tormé, being a serious jazz composer, dismissed the song as overly commercial, but realized it would be his legacy, calling it "his annuity."

Like Irving Berlin, Tormé had many musical gifts— singing, playing drums, composing, and arranging. Tormé, too, began writing and performing at an early age and became quickly successful. "The Christmas Song" became a hit when Nat King Cole recorded it in 1946.

The song has been recorded by the likes of Tony Bennett, Michael Bolton, Garth Brooks, and Big Bird from Sesame Street.

"White Christmas." "The Christmas Song." Both nostalgic and snuggle-by-the-fire songs.

So snuggle by the fire (or anywhere) if you can with your loved ones this holiday. But thank God for them wherever they are.

I give thanks to my God for every remembrance of you. (Phil. 1:3)

Say What?

Tradition is a funny thing. Songs, for instance, and more specifically Christmas carols, hang around for centuries and at least some of us aren't sure what they mean.

Two carols come to mind that need a little research and explanation: "Good King Wenceslas" and "I Saw Three Ships." Hopefully now we can sing these old favorites with new understanding.

> Good King Wenceslas looked out,
> upon the Feast of Stephen,
> when the snow lay round about,
> deep and crisp and even:
> brightly shone the moon that night,
> though the frost was cruel,
> when a poor man came in sight,
> gathering winter fuel.

Wenceslas wasn't really a king but apparently he was a good man as the song implies.

Wenceslas's father was the Duke of Bohemia (now part of the Czech Republic). Although his mother was a pagan, Wenceslas became a Christian like his father. When his father died, Wenceslas was too young to take his rightful place as duke. For several years, Wenceslas's mother ruled under a regency provision. During this time, Wenceslas went to live with his grandmother who brought Christian priests and bishops into their home to teach the boy the Bible. When Wenceslas turned eighteen, he became Duke of Bohemia, and for a few short years the small country flourished. His subjects knew Wenceslas as a good man—kind and benevolent. However, his brother, Boleslav, became jealous of the duke's popularity and devised a successful plot to kill Wenceslas.

The story of the good duke was passed down through generations until a nineteenth-century Czech poet wrote down his tribute. A British writer, John Mason Neale, translated the lyric into English that we now know as "Good King Wenceslas." A thirteenth-century spring carol lends its tune to this song.

The Feast of Stephen is a reference to an old Christian holiday celebrating the life of the first Christian martyr, Stephen. On that day, usually December 26, employers and other superiors would give gifts to their servants and employees. In many countries in Europe, this tradition has lasted but it is often called Boxing Day.

Though Wenceslas was not really a king, he exemplified the nature of Christ with his goodness and benevolent spirit.

As you celebrate this season, and perhaps sing this enigmatic song (which has many more, yet unfamiliar verses), think of ways to carry on this tradition of blessing someone else with kindness in the name of the Lord.

I saw three ships come sailing in
On Christmas day, on Christmas day;
I saw three ships come sailing in
On Christmas day in the morning.

And what was in those ships all three,
On Christmas day, on Christmas day?
And what was in those ships all three,
On Christmas day in the morning?

Our Savior Christ and His lady,
On Christmas day, on Christmas day;
Our Savior Christ and His lady,
On Christmas day in the morning.

Yuletide Blessings

Pray whither sailed those ships all three,
On Christmas day, on Christmas day?
Pray whither sailed those ships all three,
On Christmas day in the morning?

O they sailed into Bethlehem,
On Christmas day, on Christmas day,
O they sailed into Bethlehem,
On Christmas day in the morning.

And all the bells on earth shall ring,
On Christmas day, on Christmas day;
And all the bells on earth shall ring,
On Christmas day in the morning.

And all the angels in Heav'n shall sing,
On Christmas day, on Christmas day;
And all the angels in Heav'n shall sing,
On Christmas day in the morning.

And all the souls on Earth shall sing,
On Christmas day, on Christmas day;
And all the souls on Earth shall sing,
On Christmas day in the morning.

Stories Behind the Carols

It has a catchy tune but what do three ships have to do with the Christmas season?

Apparently the song had such transient roots (English travelling minstrels) that it's impossible to know exactly its intended meaning.

Some believe that the three ships refer to sailing vessels that brought relics and the remains of the Magi to Germany in the twelfth century. Others believe that it represents the Holy Trinity—The Father, The Son, and The Holy Spirit. Still some have said that the three ships were for the Holy Family (Jesus, Mary, and Joseph).

The third verse definitely refers to our Lord and His mother, Mary.

But no one can explain verse five. Bethlehem is landlocked and therefore sailing ships would have a hard time sailing into there. The nearest body of water to Bethlehem is the Dead Sea about twenty miles away.

So, this song has survived not because of its deep theology, profound message, or even its geographical accuracy. Just let it be a reminder (as the last three verses suggest) that heaven and earth proclaimed that Christ has come. And then rejoice!

A Rebel's Carol

He was considered a radical in his day. At his father's knee, Isaac Watts learned a passion for Scripture but he also learned religious nonconformist ways. Dissenters, they were called in eighteenth-century England because they refused to worship or serve in the Church of England, were not allowed to attend certain schools, hold public office, or even study law.

Isaac, who was a child prodigy when it came to writing, was challenged by his father to step out of the tradition that allowed only biblical psalms to be sung in worship and to write his own lyrics. Young Isaac took the challenge and in his lifetime he penned over 600 hymns, many of which are still used today. Isaac Watts has been called the "Father of Modern Hymnody." Among his greatest hymn titles are "When I Survey the Wondrous Cross," "Am I a Soldier of the Cross?" "I Sing the Mighty Power of God," "When I Can Read My Title Clear," "Alas and Did My Savior Bleed," and of course, "Joy to the World."

Joy to the world! the Lord is come;
Let earth receive her King.
Let ev'ry heart prepare Him room,
And heav'n and nature sing,
And heaven and nature sing,
And heaven, and heaven, and nature sing.

Joy to the world! the Saviour reigns;
Let men their songs employ;
While fields and floods, rocks, hills, and plains
Repeat the sounding joy.
Repeat the sounding joy
Repeat, repeat the sounding joy.

No more let sins and sorrows grow,
Nor thorns infest the ground;
He comes to make His blessings flow
Far as the curse is found.
Far as the curse is found
Far as, far as the curse is found.

He rules the world with truth and grace,
And makes the nations prove
The glories of His righteousness,
And wonders of His love,

And wonders of His love,
And wonders, wonders, of His love.

Watts's hymns were controversial at first in the established church, but after awhile they became accepted throughout the English-speaking world. Later the early American colonial church welcomed the new songs, as immigrants brought them over from the old world. In fact, the hymnbooks of the churches in New England during the time of the American Revolution were largely filled with the songs written by Isaac Watts. It is said that during the war, while American colonists were engaged in battle with British soldiers, they ran out of wadding for their muskets. A pastor, allegedly, who was nearby ran into the church and gathered up the hymnbooks. He then began to tear out the pages and give them to the soldiers to be used as wadding. Then he yelled out, "Give 'em Watts, boys!" Supposedly this is where the adage "give 'em watt for" came from.

Psalm 98 inspired "Joy to the World."

Sing a new song to the Lord,
for He has performed wonders;
His right hand and holy arm
have won Him victory.

The Lord has made His victory known;
He has revealed His righteousness
in the sight of the nations.
He has remembered His love
and faithfulness to the house of Israel;
all the ends of the earth
have seen our God's victory.
Shout to the Lord, all the earth;
be jubilant, shout for joy, and sing.
Sing to the Lord with the lyre,
with the lyre and melodious song.
With trumpets and the blast of the ram's horn
shout triumphantly
in the presence of the Lord, our King.
Let the sea and all that fills it,
the world and those who live in it, resound.
Let the rivers clap their hands;
let the mountains shout together for joy before the Lord,
for He is coming to judge the earth.
He will judge the world righteously
and the peoples fairly.

Oddly, Watts's intention was to write lyrics about
Christ's second coming, not His first appearance at

Bethlehem. However, when the lyric was paired with a tune written by George Frideric Handel, it became not only popular but perhaps the most beloved Christmas carol of all time. Now look at the lyrics again and see it in light of its original intent—to announce Christ's return to earth.

Tales of Yore

Yuletide Tales of War

War rarely takes a holiday. Not even Christmas.

However, here are some stories during wartime that exhibit peace on earth in the midst of chaos:

1. The Christmas Rebellion

It's sometimes referred to as the Baptist War because a Baptist preacher named Samuel Sharpe led the uprising that started it. It was Christmas Day 1831 in the British-owned island of Jamaica located in the West Indies. The island was sometimes referred to as a "plantocracy" which meant that it was dominated by the white, wealthy plantation owners. And at that time in history such sugarcane plantations in the Caribbean were extremely successful. However, no plantations would have succeeded without the work of hundreds of thousands of slaves.

The rebels' demands were simple: more freedom and a working wage (only half of what freed laborers made). Sixty thousand (of the 300,000 total on the island) were part of a strike that began on Christmas Day. The slaves were determined to hold out until their demands were met. The plantation owners refused to accommodate the slaves, and after ten days a full-scale war broke out. British forces were able to contain the violence and suppress the rebellion with little bloodshed. However, the Jamaican government and the plantocracy were not satisfied. The rebellion had caused a delay in the sugarcane harvest thus cutting into plantation profits. In retaliation their masters killed almost 500 slaves. Samuel Sharpe was among those executed. He said, "I would rather die in yonder gallows, than live for a minute more in slavery."

When word of the rebellion and the aftermath slaughter reached abolitionists in British Parliament, they escalated their efforts to end slavery for good in the realm. By 1838, most slaves under British rule, including those in Jamaica, were emancipated.

2. A Truly Silent Night

The Germans started it.

The Great War, the War to End All Wars (now known to us as World War I) had been raging for five months in late 1914. On one side were Germany, Austria-Hungary, the Ottoman Empire, and others. On the other were France, England, Russia, and later the United States and others. Neither side had made much headway in defeating the other. A five-hundred-mile stretch of territory that ran through Flanders (Belgium, France, and the Netherlands) was called the Western Front.

Early in December of that year Pope Benedict XV made a public plea to both factions in the war. He asked "that the guns may fall silent at least upon the night the angels sang." However, commanding officers on both sides ignored the Pope's request and were determined to fight on—Christmas or not.

Nevertheless, on Christmas Eve 1914, German soldiers in the trenches caught the holiday spirit. They lit candles and hung them from evergreen trees. They hoisted banners that read, "We not shoot, you not shoot." Not knowing what to think, the British soldiers held their positions. Finally a German soldier dared venture into "no man's land," the field that separated the two battle trenches. A single voice began to sing:

Stille Nacht. Heilige Nacht.
Alles Schlaft, einsam wacht

(Silent Night, Holy Night
All is calm, all is bright.)

British soldiers answered with antiphonal greetings. Before too long more soldiers on either side left their trenches and began presenting small gifts to each other and exchanging handshakes. One British soldier wrote: "I wouldn't have missed that unique and weird Christmas Day for anything. . . . I spotted a German officer, some sort of lieutenant I should think, and being a bit of a collector, I intimated to him that I had taken a fancy to some of his buttons. . . . I brought out my wire clippers and, with a few deft snips, removed a couple of his buttons and put them in my pocket. I then gave him two of mine in exchange. . . ."

News spread down the lines. From Christmas Day until well into the New Year, regiments along the battle lines joined in with similar gestures of goodwill, much to the chagrin of their commanders. (One notable dissenter was a young corporal named Adolf Hitler.)

Referring to that short unofficial ceasefire, another soldier reported, "I remember the silence, the eerie sound of silence. Only the guards were on duty. We all went outside the farm buildings and just stood listening. And, of course, thinking of people back home. All I'd heard for two months in the trenches was the hissing, cracking, and whining of bullets in flight, machine gun fire, and distant German voices. But there was a dead silence that morning, right across the land as far as you could see. We shouted 'Merry Christmas,' even though nobody felt merry. The silence ended early in the afternoon and the killing started again. It was a short peace in a terrible war."

These two Christmas war stories bring heartwarming and inspiring sentiments. One coming from a passion for freedom; another coming from a yearning for peace. But the Prince of Peace, Jesus, had already come to wage His own war against sin and despair that has been around since Eden. The peace He gives, however, is not the absence of conflict but the serenity of spirit that the apostle Paul describes as "the peace that passes human understanding."

Yuletide Blessings

Today our world is full of conflict and oppression without any external sign or hope of relief. This makes knowing the Prince of Peace even more beautiful.

Jesus spoke of freedom in John 8:34–36:

> *"I assure you: Everyone who commits sin is a slave of sin. A slave does not remain in the household forever, but a son does remain forever. Therefore, if the Son sets you free, you really will be free."*

Regarding peace, Jesus told His disciples,

> *"Peace I leave with you. My peace I give to you. I do not give as the world gives. Your heart must not be troubled or fearful." (John 14:27)*

Home for the Holidays

If you are traveling by airplane for the holidays, this story (though some call part of it legend) might have more significance than others.

Man had been fascinated with flight since the beginning of time. As far back as the ancient Chinese in the fourth century BC, humans have tried to harness the wind and fly above the ground like birds. A kite was his first attempt at flight, though somewhat unsatisfying because he could only observe from the ground.

Leonardo da Vinci in the mid-fifteenth century drew more than one hundred designs for a flying machine, but da Vinci was often ahead of his time in so many ways.

Then in the late nineteenth century, the manned glider was invented, but man's flight was controlled by the wind itself. Many glider flights ended in tragedy because the pilot had little or no control of his direction.

It was not until just before Christmas, December 17, 1903, that Wilbur and Orville Wright of Dayton, Ohio, perfected the design for a true flying machine.

Yuletide Blessings

By trade the brothers were bicycle and printing press builders. Both of these were not only noble professions but lucrative as well. They could have been very satisfied with their careers. But they dreamed bigger. Using the research of many others before them, the sons of Milton and Susan Wright, camped out on the eastern seaboard at Kitty Hawk, North Carolina, for three summers. There they worked on a "fixed-wing" flight design. After two summers, however, the brothers had become discouraged. They were sure that Man would someday fly, but that he would never fly during their lifetime. Fortunately the men did not give up. In the summer of 1903 after building a gasoline-powered engine that turned propellers, Orville and Wilbur decided to stay past their usual season as the fall temperatures started to plummet. They decided to keep trying despite the weather and the coming holidays. On that December morning, Orville piloted the lightweight spruce-constructed muslin-surfaced *Wright Flyer I* off the ground for fifty-nine seconds with Wilbur running along beside. The flying machine's altitude reached ten feet.

This story is a fact. But the story within the story that makes this account worthy of this publication has been touted as an urban legend. No matter, it is one tale that has a deep lesson for us all at this time of year.

Tales of Yore

After Wilbur and Orville made their momentous flight, they naturally wanted to share the news with their family back home in Dayton, Ohio. They sent a telegram to their sister Katherine telling her of the flight and that they would be home to celebrate Christmas. When Katherine excitedly ran to the newspaper office with the news, she was surprised when the editor looked at the message and exclaimed, "Oh great, the boys will be home for Christmas." The legend part of this story may be that the editor published an article in the next morning's paper that read, "Popular Local Bicycle Merchants Home for the Holidays." No such headline is archived in the *Dayton Daily News*, however.

The point is that the editor supposedly missed the impact of the message. Excited that his friends would be home for the holidays, he ignored the biggest news of the century. Man had flown!

In the excitement and preparations for Christmas, it's easy to miss the point of the season. God had come to earth. No matter what else you might hold dear at Christmas, don't miss the reason why Jesus came: to give us eternal access to our heavenly Father.

God Bless Us Everyone

The world needed a little Christmas, and British author Charles Dickens gave it to them.

He originally planned to write it as a pamphlet entitled "An Appeal to the People of England, on behalf of the Poor Man's Child." Its purpose was to incite outrage at the child labor conditions, poverty, and illiteracy that came with England's Industrial Revolution. Dickens decided that a novel (or novella in this case) could have more impact, as it would perhaps summon more readers than a pamphlet. He was right. The book *A Christmas Carol* was published on December 19, 1843, and it became immediately popular. As hoped, his story exposed greed and want, compelling readers to give more and do more for the disadvantaged.

The book was divided into five chapters or staves (or stanzas like a song), which gives the book its name.

The first stanza is the introduction of the main characters: Ebenezer Scrooge, his quite-dead business partner Jacob Marley, Scrooge's long-suffering employee Bob Cratchit and family, and Ebenezer's nephew Fred.

The miserly recluse Scrooge owns a London lending house in England's Victorian Era. He is not necessarily dishonest but is apparently charging high interest on loans making them next to impossible to repay. In addition to bilking his clients, he hordes every penny he makes. He even works (and forces his employee to work) in a cold office because he is too stingy to add more fuel to the fire. Scrooge's home, also, is dark and cold for the same reason.

When Jacob Marley's ghost appears to Ebenezer on Christmas Eve pointing out Scrooge's stinginess, he responds with his usual "Bah! Humbug!" At the end of the first stanza, Scrooge is warned that he will see the error of his ways through the appearance of three more ghosts: Christmas Past, Christmas Present, and Christmas Yet-To-Come.

At the beginning of the second stanza, Scrooge is awakened by the appearance of a rather pleasant apparition that takes Scrooge back to his childhood where he sees himself as a happy carefree boy. The vision begins merry and innocent enough but as time in his past progresses, Scrooge sees how he is hardened by his circumstances and his choices to care more for money than for his relationships. The love of his life, Belle, decides not to marry Ebenezer because of his growing obsession with money. Scrooge further hardens his heart and resigns himself to a lifetime of bachelorhood. That is how the second stanza ends.

The third stanza centers on the Ghost of Christmas Present's revelation to Scrooge. These scenes are of the merry holiday celebrations going on in two homes: one in the parlor of Scrooge's only living relative, Fred; and the humble celebrating happening in the meager home of Scrooge's employee, Cratchit. In both households Scrooge is referred to as the heartless curmudgeon that he is, but still Ebenezer is unmoved. As this stanza closes, Scrooge becomes aware of and slightly concerned about Cratchit's youngest child, Tiny Tim. A cripple, the boy cannot receive the proper diet or medical care that he needs because of his family's poverty.

It is the fourth stanza that truly troubles Ebenezer Scrooge. He is faced with a future that includes his own mortality and the true worth of the treasures he has amassed during his lifetime. He is most disturbed by the death of Tiny Tim. Scrooge is so frightened by the scenes of his future that he begs for mercy.

When the fifth and final stanza begins, Scrooge awakens to find that it is Christmas morning and the reader finds that Scrooge has not only realized his selfishness but has repented and changed his ways.

The classic *A Christmas Carol* has never gone out of print and it has been adapted as a stage play and numerous movies including animated versions. The story has been made into an opera, a ballet, a Broadway musical, a mime starring Marcel Marceau, and an orchestral composition.

As Dickens predicted, the work of fiction had far more effect on societal reform than any pamphlet. The novella sparked awareness of poverty and greed. It set off a trend of charitable giving especially at Christmastime. One London magazine said that the book caused readers to open their hearts and hands to charity. All over the world, the book, as it became popular, spawned generous giving campaigns.

The last line of the story is this greeting from Tiny Tim: "God bless us everyone." The beauty and innocence of a child.

In one of Isaiah's greatest messianic prophecies, the future impact of a Child is expressed:

Yuletide Blessings

From Isaiah 11:2–4, 6:

The Spirit of the LORD will rest on Him—
a Spirit of wisdom and understanding,
a Spirit of counsel and strength,
a Spirit of knowledge and of the fear of the LORD.
His delight will be in the fear of the LORD.
He will not judge
by what He sees with His eyes,
He will not execute justice
by what He hears with His ears,
but He will judge the poor righteously
and execute justice for the oppressed of the land. . . .
The wolf will live with the lamb,
and the leopard will lie down with the goat.
The calf, the young lion, and the fatling will be together,
and a child will lead them.

Classic Holiday Shows

A Charlie Brown Christmas

"You can't read from the Bible on network television!"

This was just one of the complaints that the CBS television network had with the animated feature *A Charlie Brown Christmas*.

It was 1965 and *Peanuts* had been a favorite newspaper comic strip for fifteen years. Charles Shultz, its creator, had done a short film with animator Bill Melendez and producer Lee Mendelson but he had never considered making a TV movie for Christmas; that is, until the producer called Schultz and said that an advertising agent for the Coca-Cola Company had suggested they create one. Within a few days, the producer and creator had written an outline for a script. It included three main chapters: 1) a sad Christmas tree, 2) a school play, and 3) ice skating.

The twenty-five-minute animated film budget was around $150,000, which even in the 1960s was quite low. The creative team of Schultz, Mendelson, and Melendez pressed on, however, until they had a full production to present to the TV network CBS.

The main complaint that the TV executives had against the film was the recitation by Linus straight out of the second chapter of the Gospel of Luke. CBS did not believe that a biblical reference, much less a direct quote from the King James Version of the Bible, was appropriate for their audience. Charles Schultz, however, begged to differ. He is quoted as saying, "If we don't tell the true meaning of Christmas, who will?" Schultz refused to delete the scene or the scene where the children sing the religious carol "Hark! The Herald Angels Sing."

But the biblical reference wasn't the only thing the network didn't like. They also didn't like that real children, not adult industry professionals, were used to record the voices on the film. (In fact, some of the children were so young that they couldn't read their lines and had to be fed them by the producer one sentence at a time.)

The third thing that did not ring true with the CBS executives was the music. Jazz musician and composer, Vince Guaraldi, had already written a song called "Linus and Lucy" for a documentary about *Peanuts* that never aired. The creative team called Guaraldi and asked him if they could use the song on the Christmas special. The composer also wrote another song for the film, "Christmastime Is Here." CBS thought the songs, especially the theme song, was too abstract and offbeat for a cartoon.

The final complaint was the absence of a "laugh track." Most comedy shows in the 1960s had laugh tracks, which were prerecorded voices laughing that were dropped into the sound to tell the TV audience when to laugh. It was to keep the pace up and light. The absence of a laugh track for *A Charlie Brown Christmas* was by design. Schultz said that he wanted his audience to laugh whenever they felt like it—or not to laugh at all if they chose. This was a very revolutionary idea in sixties' television.

Under pressure by the sponsor Coca-Cola, the network finally conceded. *A Charlie Brown Christmas* would be aired on a Thursday night, December 9, 1965. More than fifteen million TV viewers saw the show, and the ratings for the show was at number two just behind *Bonanza*.

The film has had some changes over the years. One is that the Coca-Cola symbols are not shown on the present version, since the soft drink company no longer sponsors it. A few more edits have been made too. But only minor ones.

The original animation, which many thought was crude, is exactly as it first appeared in 1965. It has now been dubbed "classic" by animators and producers since.

At Christmastime we focus on those who believed that the Infant in Bethlehem was the Messiah: Mary, Joseph, shepherds, Wise Men. But what about those who didn't believe? Some just couldn't see the potential lying in a manger or later walking the earth.

Since Charles Schultz was a believer, he may have resonated a little with Jesus as His skeptics passed Him over too. Network naysayers were just as blind as stubborn Pharisees to the treasure that was right in front of them.

Classic Holiday Shows

An angel of the Lord suddenly appeared to him
[Joseph] in a dream, saying, "Joseph, son of David,
don't be afraid to take Mary as your wife, because
what has been conceived in her is by the Holy Spirit.
She will give birth to a son, and you are to name
Him Jesus, because He will save His people from their
sins." (Matt. 1:20–21)

It's a Wonderful Story

It started with a short story that no one would publish.

"The Greatest Gift" written by Philip Van Doren Stern was about a despondent man who, at the point of suicide, is visited by his guardian angel who shows the desperate man what the world would have been like if he had not been born. No publisher wanted Stern's story, so after several years he published it himself—in the form of a Christmas card he sent to his friends and family.

A Hollywood film producer eventually saw the card, liked the story, and bought the rights from the author for $10,000. After a couple of years with no acceptable screenplay adaptation in the works, the rights were sold again to the studio where veteran film director, Frank Capra, worked. Capra saw the potential in the story and began working on the film, as we know it today: *It's a Wonderful Life*.

The fictitious town of Bedford Falls, New York, was the setting and the time was post-World War II. Jimmy

Stewart wasn't the first choice for George Bailey, the male lead. Cary Grant was a contender and so was Henry Fonda. Ginger Rogers, a popular starlet back then that every filmmaker wanted to cast, was offered the part of female lead Mary Hatch, but she turned it down because she said it was dull. Olivia de Havilland (of *Gone with the Wind* fame) also turned down the role. Donna Reed finally landed the part. Adding Lionel Barrymore as the greedy, conniving banker Henry Potter, the rest of the cast fell into place. Even Carl Switzer (better known as "Alfalfa" in the *Little Rascals* series) had a small role (without his signature cowlick) as Freddie, a schoolmate of Mary's.

The film was released just in time for Christmas 1946. At best, the film had mixed reviews with most of the critics giving it a "thumbs down." They didn't so much hate it as they dismissed it, dubbing it too sentimental, unrealistic, and too predictable. It did get nominated for five Academy Awards that year but won none.

It's a Wonderful Life did gain some attention the next year, however, from the FBI. Six months after the movie released, it was caught up in McCarthyism politics as the bureau declared that the movie might have ties to

Communism. They claimed that the character Henry Potter portrayed bankers as Scrooge-like and crooked, and they thought the film had a subtle, but subversive Communist bent.

The movie took ninety days to shoot. The set for Bedford Falls was built in California's San Fernando Valley and then filmed during a summer heat wave. In fact, in some of the outdoor winter scenes Jimmy Stewart is heavily perspiring.

To create a snow scene on a Hollywood set in those days involved crushed corn flakes to replicate snow. Even though movies were shot in black and white back then, the flakes were painted white and worked just fine. They floated just like snowflakes. However, once they fell to the ground, they made a distracting crunchy sound when the actors walked on them. Most filmmakers dealt with the noise by overdubbing dialogue to overcome the background crunching noise. Capra didn't want to overdub the voices so he asked his crew to create silent snow. They did so by using Foamite, a material used in fire extinguishers, with sugar, water, and even soap flakes. This formula called "chemical snow" became a movie industry standard.

Classic Holiday Shows

It's a Wonderful Life has now joined the prestigious ranks of the greatest movies ever made. And it all started with a story no one wanted to hear.

Dance Like It's Christmas

It was not a hit when it premiered on December 18, 1892, in St. Petersburg, Russia.

The Nutcracker was a ballet based on the story *The Nutcracker and the Mouse King* (written by E. T .A. Hoffman in 1816). Two well-known choreographers were asked to stage it, French novelist Alexander Dumas (*The Count of Monte Cristo* and *The Three Musketeers*) wrote the adaption for stage, and the beloved Russian composer Peter Tchaikovsky wrote the musical score. But the performance got scathing reviews from the critics. It was "boring," "amateurish," and the scene transitions were "choppy." With such a team of writers and composers, how could it have opened so dismally?

Its season was yet to come.

Tchaikovsky had recently written the musical score to another ballet, *The Sleeping Beauty,* which was an immediate success. When *The Nutcracker* did not fare as well, the composer was determined to at least salvage the music. He put together a 20-minute presentation he called *The Nutcracker Suite.* He included "Dance of the Sugar Plum Fairy," "Waltz of the Flowers," and "The Russian Dance" in the suite.

Years went by and the ballet had hit-and-miss performances each with some change that the stagers hoped would improve the show. It was not until the late 1960s in America that the ballet was accepted as a classic. It is now performed all over the world each Christmas.

The performances still have variations. Some ballet companies omit certain scenes and others adapt the original show to their own tastes. But the basic story remains. It is Christmas Eve and Clara, a young child, is helping her family decorate their Christmas tree when a family friend, who is the village toymaker, enters bearing gifts for her family. Of all the gifts, Clara is most drawn to a very ordinary wooden nutcracker. When her brother Fritz breaks the nutcracker, Clara is terribly upset. During that night while the family is sleeping, Clara returns to the parlor to see if she can repair it. At the stroke of midnight, the nutcracker comes to life along with other characters—mice and life-sized toys. The nutcracker is in danger of being killed by the mice, but Clara rescues it. The nutcracker turns into a handsome prince who takes her on an adventure to yet another fantasy.

Yuletide Blessings

Since 1932, the Rockettes have performed their Christmas Spectacular at the largest indoor theater in the world—Radio City Music Hall. Millionaire John D. Rockefeller Jr. who was determined to leave a lasting impact on the city of New York built the theater during the dark days of the Great Depression. By building the great hall, he brought hope and inspiration to so many during a difficult time. Today more than one million people see the Christmas Spectacular annually, and the show has expanded to a travelling version that can be seen in many cities across the country.

Though the show changes slightly from year to year, there are two standards that do not change. The Parade of the Wooden Soldiers, where the dancers re-create a slow toppling of the life-sized soldiers, is a favorite. The bigger-than-life Living Nativity Scene has also been included every year since the inception of the show. Live animals, elegant costumes, and special effects exaggerate the story of Christ's birth, but it does pay due homage to the King of kings.

Your Own Christmas Story

Write Your Story as a Blessing

It may be a past holiday that you were far from home—or you were home and loved ones were not.

It could be a Christmas season when you were financially strapped, or it could be about a time you received a gift that you had only dreamed about.

It doesn't matter what memory or memories you choose. Write them down here, in the pages provided, and share them with those you love. Pass your story to another generation and pray that someone will be blessed by your insights.

Yuletide Blessings

Notes

Yuletide Blessings

Notes

Bibliography

Emurian, Ernest K. *Stories of Yuletide*. Grand Rapids, MI: Baker Book House, 1960.

Trimiew, Anna. *Bible Almanac: Understanding the World of the Bible.* Lincolnwood, IL: Publications International, 1997.

Howard, Jr., David M. *Fascinating Bible Facts.* Lincolnwood, IL: Publications International, 1997.

MacArthur, John. *God's Gift of Christmas.* Nashville, TN: Thomas Nelson, Inc. 2006.

Emurian, Ernest K. *Stories of Christmas Carols.* Grand Rapids, MI: Baker Book House, 1958.

Snow, Michael C., *Oh, Holy Night: The Peace of 1914.* Nappanee, IN: Evangel Press, 2009.

Butler, Trent C. *Holman Bible Dictionary.* Nashville, TN: Holman Bible Publishers, 1991.

Unger, Merrill F. *Unger's Bible Dictionary.* Chicago: The Moody Bible Institute, 1974.

Gower, Ralph, *The New Manners and Customs of Bible Times.* Chicago: Moody Publishers, 1987.

Hertha Pauli: *Silent Night. A Story of a Song.* New York: Alfred A. Knopf, 1943.

Morrison, Dorothy. *Yule: A Celebration of Light and Warmth.* Woodbury, MN: Llewellyn Publications, 2000.

Tomalin, Claire. *Charles Dickens: A Life.* New York: The Penguin Press, 2011.

Bloom, Nate. *The Jews Who Wrote Christmas Songs.* Newton Upper Falls, MA: InterfaithFamily, 2006.

http://nethymnal.org/htm/o/l/olittle.htm

Bairnsfather, Bruce, *Bullets and Billets,* Project Gutenberg, 2009

Mendelson, Lee *A Charlie Brown Christmas: The Making of a Tradition* , Harper Paperbacks, 2005

Fisher, J. *Nutcracker Nation: How an Old World Ballet Became a Christmas Tradition in the New World,* New Haven: Yale University Press, 2003

www.cyberhymnal.org.

www.rockettes.com.